A *DISCIPLESHIP JOURNAL* BIBLE • STUDY ON
LOVING GOD

GROWING DEEPER WITH GOD

BY SUSAN NIKAIDO

NAVPRESS
BRINGING TRUTH TO LIFE
P.O. Box 35001, Colorado Springs, Colorado 80935

OUR GUARANTEE TO YOU

We believe so strongly in the message of our books that we are making this quality guarantee to you. If for any reason you are disappointed with the content of this book, return the title page to us with your name and address and we will refund to you the list price of the book. To help us serve you better, please briefly describe why you were disappointed. Mail your refund request to: NavPress, P.O. Box 35002, Colorado Springs, CO 80935.

The Navigators is an international Christian organization. Our mission is to reach, disciple, and equip people to know Christ and to make Him known through successive generations. We envision multitudes of diverse people in the United States and every other nation who have a passionate love for Christ, live a lifestyle of sharing Christ's love, and multiply spiritual laborers among those without Christ.

NavPress is the publishing ministry of The Navigators. NavPress publications help believers learn biblical truth and apply what they learn to their lives and ministries. Our mission is to stimulate spiritual formation among our readers.

ISBN 1-57683-153-1

Cover illustration by The Schuna Group, Inc.

Unless otherwise identified, all Scripture quotations in this publication are taken from the *HOLY BIBLE: NEW INTERNATIONAL VERSION®* (NIV®), copyright © 1973, 1978, 1984 by International Bible Society. Used by permission of Zondervan Publishing House. All rights reserved. Other versions used include: the *New American Standard Bible* (NASB), © The Lockman Foundation 1960, 1962, 1963, 1968, 1971, 1972, 1973, 1975, 1977; *The Living Bible* (TLB), copyright © 1971, used by permission of Tyndale House Publishers, Inc., Wheaton, IL 60189, all rights reserved; the *Amplified New Testament* (AMP), © The Lockman Foundation 1954, 1958; and the *New King James Version* (NKJV), copyright © 1979, 1980, 1982, 1990, Thomas Nelson Inc., Publishers.

Printed in the United States of America

2 3 4 5 6 7 8 9 10 11 / 07 06 05 04 03 02 01

FOR A FREE CATALOG OF
NAVPRESS BOOKS & BIBLE STUDIES,
CALL 1-800-366-7788 (USA)
OR 1-416-499-4615 (CANADA)

Contents

Introduction

Intimacy with God

Many Christians talk about their "personal relationship" with God. For many of us, however, the "personal" part of that relationship seems to be missing. We want to know God in a deeply personal, intimate way, but that's not what we experience. How can we develop intimacy with God?

Over the years, *Discipleship Journal* has published a number of articles about the importance of a deeply personal, intimate walk with God and how Christians can develop that kind of a relationship with their heavenly Father. This study compiles some of those significant articles and combines them with discussion questions and innovative learning activities that can help you experience an intimate relationship with God.

As you read, study, and interact with the articles, questions, and activities, you'll examine the following questions about intimacy with God:

- What are the keys to intimacy with God?
- How can you learn to spend time with God?
- How well do you know God?
- How can you experience God's love?
- What are the hindrances to knowing God?
- Are you really listening to God?
- How can you keep your passion for God alive?
- What can you do to jump-start your spiritual battery?

How This Study Guide Works

This *Discipleship Journal Bible Study* may look a little different from study guides you have used in the past. In addition to the Scriptures that you'll be looking at in each session, we've combed through issues of *Discipleship Journal* magazine and selected some of the best articles on a variety of topics essential to living life as a disciple of Christ in today's world.

This combination of Scripture texts and the sharpened insights of experienced communicators should give you plenty to contemplate as you discover what it means to follow Jesus in your life situation.

We have also put more emphasis on thinking about, praying over, meditating on, and wrestling with the meaning of a few key Scripture passages than on quickly looking at as many verses as possible. You'll sometimes find multiple questions about a single passage that are intended to help you understand what the passage says and how it applies to you personally. The idea is to help you to be a "doer" of the Word and not merely a "hearer" (James 1:22).

Not all questions incorporate specific verses of Scripture, but they all are intended to help you think through what it means to apply biblical truth. Sometimes that will involve changing the way you *think*, and often it will mean changing the way you *act*.

This study guide is designed to be used either individually or in a small group setting. (Your experience will likely be enhanced by the input, perspective, and prayers of other like-minded believers.) Even if you work on this study on your own, we encourage you to share your insights and discoveries with someone who can help "sharpen" you in your walk with God (see Proverbs 27:17).

Our prayer is that God's Word will both challenge and encourage you as you seek to follow Him "with all your heart and with all your soul and with all your mind and with all your strength" (Mark 12:30).

1

Keys to Intimacy

The following article, entitled **"Becoming a Friend of God"** by **Cynthia Heald** (excerpted from Issue 54), explores the process of developing intimacy with God. As you read through the article, highlight any points that stand out to you. Then respond to the questions and exercises.

D Longing for His Friendship

Intimacy with God. The prospect thrills us—and at the same time frustrates us.

How few people we know, or even know of, who experience the kind of closeness with God that our hearts long for. Even in Scripture only a handful of people seemed to have a special relationship with the Father.

When we read the words of saints like Hudson Taylor, Amy Carmichael, D. L. Moody, and the writers of the great hymns, we find a spiritual depth that not many of us experience. Is this special communion with the Lord reserved for a favored few? Is it presumptuous to consider that God Himself would be our intimate friend?

1. What does the phrase "intimacy with God" mean to you? How would you describe what it means to a friend?

2. Check the statement that comes closest to describing your experience of intimacy with God.

    ☐ The thought of being close to God is scary to me.
    ☐ Intimacy with God is something I long for but have never experienced.
    ☐ I have experienced intimacy with God during certain periods of my life, but not consistently.
    ☐ I experience intimacy with God most of the time.
    ☐ Other:

3. Think back to those times when you have felt closest to God. List the circumstances or conditions that caused you to be especially close to Him.

4. Do you know anyone, or have you read about anyone, who seems to be especially close to God? In what ways do you wish you could be like that person?

5. How do you think that person developed and maintained intimacy with God?

God the Initiator

Very simply, intimacy is close or confidential friendship. And God, far from making it mysterious or unobtainable, has sought that kind of relationship with us from the beginning: "Let us make man in our image, in our likeness" (Genesis 1:26). He revealed Himself to the patriarchs and prophets; He personally led the Israelites in the wilderness by cloud and by fire.

God's ultimate invitation to fellowship with Him was in sending His Son to pay the price for our sin so that we who believe could be called His children. To seal His presence in us, He sent His Holy Spirit to dwell within us.

God continually invites us to respond to His love and desire for fellowship. He longs to love us as only He can, and He wants us to know Him in all of His fullness. His commandment to us is "Love the LORD your God with all your heart and with all your soul and with all your strength" (Deuteronomy 6:5). He wants us to be intimate with Him. Why, then, do so few of us experience a deep love relationship with God? What does it take to know Him as an intimate friend?

---

6. Reflect on the statement "God wants us to be intimate with Him." Why do you think this is difficult for many Christians to truly believe?

7. Read the following passages about how God views us. Pick your favorite one and summarize what it tells you about God's love for you.

    □ Psalm 139:13-18

    □ Zephaniah 3:17

    □ John 3:16

    □ Romans 5:6-8

    □ 1 Peter 2:9

    □ 1 John 3:1

8. What did God promise in Jeremiah 29:13?

9. a. With how much of your heart have you sought God in the last week? Draw a simple heart below and color in the portion that represents your answer.

b. Give an example of what you think it means to seek God "with all your heart."

Deep Desire

Those saints, past and present, who have enjoyed exceptional closeness with God are first of all those who have deeply longed for it.

David's longing for God was insatiable. Even when he was pursued by enemies, he did not seek deliverance or a change in circumstances; he sought God. He wrote, "O God, you are my God, earnestly I seek you; my soul thirsts for you, my body longs for you, in a dry and weary land where there is no water" (Psalm 63:1).

The apostle Paul counted "everything as loss compared to the possession of the priceless privilege—the overwhelming preciousness, the surpassing worth and supreme advantage—of knowing Christ Jesus my Lord" (Philippians 3:8, AMP). The only intimacy that mattered to Paul was intimacy with his Lord. He had become his focus, his goal in life, his chief desire.

In *Enjoying Intimacy with God*, J. Oswald Sanders observed,

> It would seem that admission to the inner circle of deepening intimacy with God is the outcome of deep desire. Only those who count such intimacy a prize worth sacrificing anything else for, are likely to attain it. If other intimacies are more desirable to us, we will not gain entry to that circle.

A desire to know the Lord and His character must be our motive for intimacy. If all I seek are His gifts or what He can do for me, I have a self-centered relationship based on God's "performance" in meeting my perceived needs. Instead, my desire to seek Him must be based on a longing just to know Him, to fellowship with Him, and to enjoy His company.

---

10. a. Many desires can pull us away from pursuing intimacy with God. Put a check mark next to any of the following that you are tempted to pursue, at the cost of your relationship with God.

☐ Success at work   ☐ Ministry
☐ Family   ☐ Leisure activities
☐ Friends   ☐ Dating
☐ Other:

   b. Circle the one area that most often prevents you from pursuing God. Why do you tend to put it before your relationship with God?

   c. What can you do to make sure it doesn't squeeze God out of your heart and your schedule?

11. Study Psalm 63:1-8. In the space below list everything you discover from this passage about seeking God.

12. What rewards did David experience as a result of seeking God?

D Dependence

In order to seek God in this way, I must be willing to admit that I am not the center of the universe, and that I am not self-sufficient. I cannot depend on anyone else but the living God to fully and consistently care about what is best for me. To earnestly seek God, I must be willing to enter into a relationship with Him on His terms by acknowledging my need and dependence upon Him. David wrote, "Find rest, O my soul, in God alone; my hope comes from him. He alone is my rock and my salvation" (Psalm 62:5-6).

In my life the greatest hindrance to developing intimacy with the Father is my bent to live my life in my own strength, to rely on my own insight, to think that I know what God wants me to do. I can easily distance myself from the Lord by trusting my feelings and my inclinations.

The psalmists knew that if they were left to their own devices, they would ultimately fail. They longed for God and God alone to be their rock and their salvation—and so must we.

13. On what or whom are you tempted to rely instead of relying on God alone?

☐ Your spouse   ☐ Your family
☐ Your spiritual leaders   ☐ Your friends
☐ Your own abilities   ☐ Your achievements
☐ Other:

14. In what condition did the apostle Paul say we can best experience the power of Christ (2 Corinthians 12:7-10)?

15. How was his perspective on weakness different from most people's thinking?

16. a. What weaknesses in your life force you to rely on God's power?

   b. Take a few moments to thank God for these opportunities to depend on Him.

D| Abiding

If I truly desire to be intimate with someone, then I plan to be with that person as much as I can. David wrote, "The one thing I want from God, the thing I seek most of all, is the privilege of . . . living in his presence every day of my life, delighting in his incomparable perfections and glory" (Psalm 27:4, TLB).

Realistically, though, how can we live in His presence every day of our lives? Psalm 91:1 tells us, "He who dwells in the shelter of the Most High will rest in the shadow of the Almighty." To dwell means to remain, abide, sit. It conveys a constancy, a continuity, a daily communion with the Lord.

The relationship spoken of here is not an erratic visitation as need dictates. Jesus taught, "I am the vine, you are the branches; he who abides in Me, and I in him, he bears much fruit; for apart from Me you can do nothing" (John 15:5, NASB). To bear the fruit of His character, which can only come from the intimacy of living with Him, we must choose to dwell in His shelter.

For me, abiding means taking the time to nurture my friendship with the Lord. It means spending special time with Him daily, reading and studying His Word and conversing with Him. It means planning mornings or days alone with Him. Since He is my confidant, it means coming to Him first with my joys, my hurts, my frustrations.

Abiding means choosing to live in His presence and realizing that He is with me wherever I go. It means continually sharing my thoughts with Him throughout the day. It means meditating on His Scriptures so that I can know Him better. It means friendship sought on the deepest level. The decision to abide commits me to a lifelong process of developing intimacy with God.

---

17. Reflect on the Scriptures quoted in the preceding paragraphs. In the space below, draw a picture or diagram of what it looks like to abide in God's presence. (Stick figures are fine!)

Ⓓ Obedience

Desiring Him and acknowledging God's rightful place in our lives are important aspects of intimacy. Yet, even with God's great love and desire for us, we cannot presume upon His character. Our God is a holy God. David wrote, "Friendship with God is reserved for those who reverence him. With them alone he shares the secrets of his promises" (Psalm 25:14, TLB).

Reverence, respect, and fear of God are essential to abiding in Him. To reverence and respect the Lord is to stand in awe of His majesty, His holiness, His power, and His glory. To fear the Lord is to be concerned about ever displeasing Him.

In Psalm 15:1-2, David described the heart of those who dwell with God. "LORD, who may dwell in your sanctuary? Who may live on your holy hill? He whose walk is blameless and who does what is righteous, who speaks the truth from his heart."

---

18. The standards in Psalm 15:1-2 seem awfully high—especially since we know that we all sin and fall short of God's standards. What do you think it means to have a "blameless" walk, to do what is "righteous," and to "speak the truth from the heart"?

Ⓓ One of the most succinct verses on intimacy with God is John 14:21: "Whoever has my commands and obeys them, he is the one who loves me. He who loves me will be loved by my Father, and I too will love him and show myself to him." If we love God and want to grow in our knowledge of Him, we will obey His commands. It is in our obedience that God discloses Himself to us. Jesus said, "You are my friends if you do what I command" (John 15:14).

If I desire to share in "the secrets of his promise," then I will choose to pursue a lifestyle of purity. Abiding in His presence will alter my thought life, my activities, my relationships.

This does not mean that I will always be blameless. Someone once said, "The essence of holiness is not that we are perfect, but that we never stop pursuing it." If I truly want to draw closer to God, then my heart's desire will be to please the Lord and to bring Him glory in all that I do.

---

19. a. Are you clinging to disobedience in any way? Is there something God wants you to do that you are failing to do? Is there something God wants you to stop doing? Reflect on the areas below, and ask God to point out any disobedience in your life.

- Marriage
- Work
- Other relationships
- Spending
- Ministry
- Speech
- Other:

- Other family
- Parenting
- Leisure activities
- Response to the poor
- Attitudes
- Thought life

b. If God reveals any sin, take some time to talk to Him about it. Tell Him how you want to change in this area, and ask Him to show you how.

D A Settled Assurance

If intimacy with God is our ardent desire, then we will diligently seek Him for the friendship that only He can provide. We will trust Him with our lives and we will choose to honor Him by desiring to live righteously before Him.

If we are willing to know the Lord in this way, what will our lives be like? Will we continually experience spiritual ecstasy? Do we need to withdraw from the demands of daily life and just sit at the feet of Jesus?

Intimacy, for me, is essentially a settled assurance that God is with me and for me, even though my feelings and circumstances may seem to deny His commitment to our relationship. It is trusting Him and His promise never to leave me or forsake me. It is knowing that He is with me in the reality of my life. It is not expecting some continual emotional assurance that He is my friend.

God does not have a secret society of intimate friends. We are as intimate with God as we choose to be. It is our desire, our abiding, our purity that will determine the depth of our intimacy with Him. Intimacy is knowing that I must sit at the feet of Jesus, so that I can walk with integrity as His friend. It is experiencing the closeness of the Lord and at other times wondering if He is near. Essentially, intimacy is abandonment of ourselves to the Lord—abandonment born out of trust and an intense longing to know the living God.

---

20. The author writes, "We are as intimate with God as we choose to be." Do you agree or disagree? Why? (See Proverbs 8:17.)

21. a. After reflecting on the following four aspects of intimacy with God, put a check mark next to the one that you feel is strongest in your life.

   ☐ Desire
   ☐ Dependence
   ☐ Abiding
   ☐ Obedience

   b. Now underline the aspect in which you feel you need the most growth. What steps could you take to grow in this area?

22. a. Which statement, Scripture passage, or thought from this session stands out to you the most?

b. Why?

c. How will you respond?

Parting Thought

God wants to be as close to us as a branch is to a vine. One is an extension of the other. It's impossible to tell where one starts and the other ends. The branch isn't connected to the vine only at the moment of bearing fruit. The gardener doesn't keep the branches in a box and then, on the day he wants grapes, glue them to the vine. No, the branch constantly draws nutrition from the vine. Separation means certain death.

—Max Lucado, from "Keeping Company with God," Issue 106

2

Spending Time with God

The following article, entitled **"Your Appointment with God: A Meeting of Two Hearts"** (excerpted from Issue 13), addresses our need to spend daily time with God. As you read, underline the points that stand out to you, then move on to the questions.

God Calls Us

Just as God sought out Adam after Adam's sin—calling, "Where are you?" (Genesis 3:9)—so He still seeks men and women today. He calls again, "Where are you?"

Having restored—at great cost to Himself—your potential for being part of His family, He now wants you to know Him intimately in a strong and ongoing way. This relationship began when you believed in Jesus Christ as your Savior, but it needs to be continually nurtured by spending quality time alone with Him.

A daily appointment with God—whether you call it a quiet time, a daily devotion, a morning watch, or something else—provides this concentrated time with Him that is so powerful and refreshing. So it is that two searching hearts can meet: the heart of God, who calls out to His child, "Where are you?" and your own heart, perhaps weary, perhaps confused, but wanting to know and experience God, and calling out to Him, "Where are You?"

1. How's your quiet time? Evaluate the time you set aside to spend alone with God, talking to Him and letting Him speak

to you through the Scriptures. Then check the statement below that represents your current situation.

☐ What quiet time?
☐ It's not as regular as I'd like it to be.
☐ I meet with God regularly, but I haven't gotten much out of it lately.
☐ I usually have a good time meeting with God, but I long for something more.
☐ It's nearly always a satisfying time of communion with God.
☐ Other:

2. How would you answer God's question, "Where are you?"

3. According to the following passages, why is spending time with God important?

    ▪ Jeremiah 31:3
    ▪ Psalm 16:11
    ▪ Psalm 19:7-11
    ▪ Psalm 62:1-2
    ▪ John 15:4

D How will you spend your time with God? One helpful way is to do these five things:
    ▪ Pray.
    ▪ Read God's Word.
    ▪ Meditate on what you read.
    ▪ Decide how to apply to your life what you have read and meditated on.
    ▪ Pray again.

As you read, don't rush. You are not merely trying to "find something," but to develop a relationship with God. Read for the pure joy of reading and allowing God to speak personally to you.

Stop reading and meditate if you feel God is speaking to you in a certain passage. Meditation involves mulling your thoughts over in your mind and heart. You might call it "thought diges-tion"—considering a biblical thought deliberately and thoroughly, providing a vital link between reading God's truth and allowing it to affect how you live.

God is seeking you. He wants personal fellowship with you, rather than your adherence to a ritual.

This next article by **Hannelore Bozeman** (excerpted from "**How to Revive Your Quiet Time**," Issue 32) offers seven suggestions for making the most of your time with God.

Ask God to Search Your Heart

We need to open the door to the attic and pray, "Search me, O God, and know my heart; test me and know my anxious thoughts. See if there is any offensive way in me, and lead me in the way everlast-ing" (Psalm 139:23-24). Then we need to listen patiently for God to reveal the clutter.

The Bible tells us that we are dwelling places of the living God. Like most houses, we tend to have an attic or a closet full of clutter. We stuff anything into it that we don't want to deal with. As long as the door is shut, we can fool ourselves into thinking the whole house is clean.

---

4.   What are some of the items in your "attic"? Grumbling? Gossip? Unforgiveness? Dishonesty? Stop now and pray David's prayer in Psalm 139. (You may want to look up this prayer in different translations and choose the one that best expresses your heart.) Be silent for a time, and allow God to speak to your heart. In the space below, write down any impressions you receive from the Lord.

5. a. Read Mark 4:1-20, taking note of the following three sins mentioned by Jesus that choke the Word of God from our hearts (Mark 4:19).

☐ Worries of this life keep us from trusting God.
☐ Deceitfulness of wealth tempts us to think we don't need Him.
☐ Desire for other things distracts us from our love for Jesus.

b. To which of those three sins are you most susceptible? Put a check mark next to it, and give a brief example below.

c. In the past, how has this sin kept God's Word from having an impact on your life?

6. a. Look up the following verses pertaining to the sin you checked in question five.

▪ Worries: Matthew 6:25-34; Philippians 4:6-7
▪ Deceitfulness of wealth: Matthew 6:19-24; 1 Timothy 6:6-10
▪ Desire for other things: Matthew 6:31-33; 1 John 2:15-17

b. What do these verses say about the futility of this sin?

7. How can you combat this sin in the future?

8. Read 1 John 1:8-10. What does the Bible promise to those who confess their sins?

9. Why is confession an important part of spending time with God?

10. How could you incorporate asking God to search your heart and a time of confession into every quiet time?

Ⅾ Seek to Know God

Recently I set aside extra time to seek the Lord for some answers about my ministry. But as I entered into His presence, I found myself drawn away from my list of questions and toward God alone. I realized that God created and redeemed me so that I could know Him, and that Jesus came to give me eternal life, which is characterized by intimate knowledge of God.

When the week drew to a close, many of my questions remained unanswered, but that didn't matter. I had experienced a deeper spiritual refreshment than ever before.

11. a. If someone asked you which of the following friends you would prefer spending time with, your answer would no doubt be obvious (check one):

☐ A friend who always comes to you with a list of things he wants from you
☐ A friend who always seeks ways to know and understand you better

b. Putting the shoe on the other foot for a moment, check the answer that best describes the way you relate to God.

12. How can you seek a deeper relationship with God? Write down three ways in which you could try to get to know God during your quiet time. Be creative! If you have trouble

coming up with ideas, think about how you would get to know a new friend or someone you were dating. Or, ask several Christian friends how they grow closer to God in their quiet times.

a.

b.

c.

D God's call to know Him extends to all believers, regardless of time pressures and obligations. The apostle Paul not only traveled frequently, founded numerous churches, and wrote half of the New Testament, but also supported himself by tent making—yet his prayer life was constant. David was a busy king, but he still sought God constantly, and his prayers—recorded in the Psalms—bless us today. Jesus ministered to people all day long but still found time for an extensive prayer life.

Begin where you are. Ask God to give you great hunger and thirst for Him. Tell Him you want to be changed. As you learn to focus on Him, reordering your priorities will become easier, until you can say with Paul, "I consider everything a loss compared to the surpassing greatness of knowing Christ Jesus my Lord" (Philippians 3:8).

God promised the Israelites, "But if . . . you seek the LORD your God, you will find him if you look for him with all your heart and with all your soul" (Deuteronomy 4:29). Rest in this promise when you seek God in your quiet times.

Thank and Praise God

The proper way to come before the King of the universe is with thanksgiving and praise (Psalm 100:4). God wants people to worship Him in spirit and in truth (John 4:23). Therefore worship is essential to entering His presence.

Study the Psalms to learn ways to worship God. Singing, shouting, clapping or raising your hands, dancing, and falling down before Him are all scriptural ways to worship. Jewish believers weren't inhibited in worship! We shouldn't be, either.

Ask the Holy Spirit to set you free, then experiment with various forms of worship when you are alone.

One special form of praise is giving God thanks and telling Him why we love Him. David frequently recounted God's mighty acts on his behalf in the Psalms. You can reflect often on what He has done for you on the Cross and in your life.

13.　For what did the following people praise God? (If you are not familiar with the story, read the related verses.)

a. Abraham's servant (Genesis 24:26-27)

b. Moses and the Israelites (Exodus 15:1-4)

c. The Israelites (Deuteronomy 8:10)

d. Naomi's friends (Ruth 4:14)

e. David (2 Samuel 22:1,47-50)

f. Solomon (1 Kings 8:56)

g. Zechariah (Luke 1:68)

14. List five things for which you could praise God today.

15. Read Psalm 145:8-20 and record in the space below every aspect of God that is worthy of worship. Underline the aspects that are most meaningful to you.

Feed Mainly on the Bible

I love Christian books and read them frequently. But when I rely more heavily on them than on the Bible, I am not feeding enough on the real food. "Man does not live on bread alone, but on every word that comes from the mouth of God" (Matthew 4:4).

If Christian literature substitutes for the Word, it does to us spiritually what junk food does physically: it spoils the appetite without providing proper nutrients for growth.

Beware the temptation to let Christian books become the main element in your spiritual diet. As useful as they are, they cannot take the place of God's written Word. It alone "is living and active and sharper than any two-edged sword, and piercing as far as the division of soul and spirit, of both joints and marrow, and able to judge the thoughts and intentions of the heart" (Hebrews 4:12, NASB).

16. a. After reading and thinking about Psalm 19:7-11, how would you summarize the benefits of spending time in God's Word?

b. Which of these benefits is most motivating to you? Why?

Ask!

"You do not have, because you do not ask God" (James 4:2). Has your study of the Bible seemed fruitless lately? Perhaps it is because you haven't asked God to teach you new and exciting things, things that will change your life.

Begin by asking, "Lord, what are You saying to me? What do You want me to do?" Seek insight on how to apply the Word in various areas of your life. The more questions you ask, the more answers you will receive.

Ask God for spiritual treasures, like learning to overcome temptation and sin, growing in Him, getting to know Him, and so on. As long as you are asking with the right motives, to please Him instead of yourself, you will receive (James 4:3; Matthew 7:7; 1 John 5:14-15).

17.   Daydream about what you would like your quiet time to be like—and about how you'd like God to use that time in your life. Let your imagination run wild. Don't be limited by thoughts such as "He'd never do that for me." Make a list of your ideas below and *ask!*

a. What I'd like my quiet time to be like:

b. How I'd like God to use my quiet time in my life:

Use a Devotional Notebook

If you write down insights from the Word, you will remember them better. But a notebook can also help you in other aspects of your devotions.

Write down what to thank and praise God for, then use your list during your worship. A record of prayers and answers will build your faith. I like to note commands the Lord gives me in my Bible reading so that I can check on my obedience later.

---

18. A wealth of devotional notebooks are available for those who are intimidated by a blank sheet of paper. Take a trip to a Christian bookstore and ask the clerk what kinds of devotional notebooks and journals they carry. Spend some time studying the various formats, then choose the one that will work best for you. Buy it, take it home, and use it! Or use a personal computer to design and print out your own notebook pages.

D Be Sure to Obey

What you do after your daily quiet time determines its quality at least as much as what you do during it. We show our love for the Lord by obeying Him in every area of life.

Disobedience to God hurts our quiet time with Him. "Do not merely listen to the word, and so deceive yourselves," wrote James. "Do what it says. Anyone who listens to the word but does not do what it says is like a man who looks at his face in a mirror and, after looking at himself, goes away and immediately forgets what he looks like. But the man who looks intently into the perfect law that gives freedom, and continues to do this, not forgetting what he has heard, but doing it—he will be blessed in what he does" (James 1:22-25).

What we learn from Scripture and in prayer during our quiet times must make a difference in our lives, or we'll soon forget it. And our consciences will make us increasingly uncomfortable because of the disrespect we show God by ignoring the commands He gives us. If we want to continually walk in a love relationship with Him, we must make it our goal to please Him by obeying Him.

---

19. a. In the quotes below, underline the phrases that Jesus used to
      describe what a person who loves Him does.

   ■ "If you love me, you will obey what I command"
      (John 14:15).

   ■ "Whoever has my commands and obeys them, he is the one
      who loves me . . . and I too will love him and show myself
      to him" (John 14:21).

   ■ "If you obey my commands, you will remain in my love"
      (John 15:10).

   ■ "You are my friends if you do what I command" (John 15:14).

   b. Are you doing these things? If not, how can you begin doing
      these things?

20. a. This week plan to spend some time each day in the Word.
      Use the following chart to record the commands you find in
      the passages you read. Then rate yourself on a scale of 1 to 3
      according to how well you are obeying those commands (1 =
      rarely obedient; 2 – sometimes obedient; 3 = regularly obedi-
      ent) In the third column, list steps you could take to obey
      God's command.

Command	Rating	How to Obey

b. Ask God if there is one particular area in which He wants you to grow in obedience. Begin to take the steps necessary to be obedient in that area. Ask a friend or family member to hold you accountable in that area.

Confess and forsake your sins; make God Himself—not spiritual knowledge—your goal; worship and praise Him; feed on the Word in ways that meet your needs; ask God for what you need; reflect on what God is doing in your life; and practice all day what you learn in communion with God in prayer and the Word, and your quiet time will become vital and exciting.

---

21. a. Look back over the seven suggestions given by the author, starting on page 21. Which two would most strengthen your devotional life in the coming week, and how?

   ▪

   ▪

   b. What will you do to incorporate these suggestions into your time with God next week?

Parting Thought

The key to a more dynamic quiet time is not finding a new method. It's enjoying a face-to-face friendship with Jesus.

—Lorraine Pintus, from "'Help! I'm Stuck in a Rut!,'" Issue 74

3

Knowing God

1. What is God like? In the space below, quickly write words and phrases that immediately come to your mind when you think of God. (Don't worry about "right" answers.)

One important way to deepen your relationship with God is to learn more about who He is and how He relates to you. The following article, entitled **"Do You Know Your Father?" by Jim Carpenter** (excerpted from Issues 50 and 51), looks at several key qualities of our heavenly Father and what He does for His children. Once you have read the article and answered the questions, compare what you learned with your response above.

D Getting to Know Him

All of us can use help in knowing our Father better. Out of my own desire to know Him, I discovered some biblical descriptions that have helped me recognize my Father.

Your Heavenly Father Is Perfect

Jesus Himself gave this description of God: "Be perfect, therefore, as your heavenly Father is perfect" (Matthew 5:48).

2. Rewrite Matthew 5:48 in your own words in the space below.

D There comes a time when every child realizes that Dad is as fallible, forgetful, and flawed as anyone else. But here's the contrast: Your heavenly Father is perfect!

Now I'll admit that the word *perfect*—so austere, so unattainable—might at first keep you at arm's length. But don't think of perfect as a total portrait of your Father. It is simply the color and light that illuminate His other features. Like love. Your Father loves you with perfect love. Or look at His wisdom. It's perfect. He is perfectly faithful and perfectly forgiving. His guidance is perfect. His plans for your life are absolutely perfect for you.

What is it that you needed in a dad when you were growing up? A listening ear? Your heavenly Father is a perfect listener. He has all eternity to focus on your needs. Was there a lack of warmth in your home because your father didn't express any tenderness toward you? Just read how your heavenly Father feels about you: "I have loved you with an everlasting love" (Jeremiah 31:3).

Not only is God perfect, but He is a perfect Father, and He is a perfect Father to you. Whatever your needs may be, He is perfectly able to meet them. He is all that you will ever need in a dad, and more.

---

3. a. Describe the ideal father. Consider what you need from a father right now as well as what you needed when you were growing up.

b. How has God been this kind of father to you?

c. Take a few minutes to thank Him for being your perfect Father.

D Your Heavenly Father Is Compassionate

"Praise be to the God and Father of our Lord Jesus Christ, the Father of compassion" (2 Corinthians 1:3).

This picture of your heavenly Father reveals that He is intensely concerned about your hurts.

4. Are there any hurts in your life right now? Check any answers that apply.

□ Rejection   □ Rebellious children
□ Illness   □ Loneliness
□ Failure   □ Depression
□ Marital problems   □ Being misunderstood
□ Other:

5. What do the following verses tell you about the Lord's compassion and how He feels about the hurts in your life?

• Psalm 145:8-9

• Isaiah 30:18

D Your pain matters to Him—even the pain that results from your sin. He doesn't rejoice when you mess up; He doesn't say, "I told you so." Instead, He feels your pain, He hurts with you.

It reminds me of a story Tim Hansel tells in his book *What Kids Need Most in a Dad*. Tim was a star athlete in high school. His team had just won the football game that would send them to the state championship. Tim decided to celebrate with his buddies by getting drunk. The young men were arrested and spent the night in jail. The next morning the parents were called to come and retrieve their sons.

> My mom and dad walked in, and I'll never forget the moment their eyes met mine. They must have been wondering if all their sacrifices had been worth it. But they never spoke a word. . . .
>
> Finally I could take the silence no longer and blurted out, "Aren't you going to say something, Dad?"
>
> After a pause that probably seemed longer than it really was, my dad finally spoke. "Sure . . . let's go have some breakfast, Son."
>
> Those were the only words he uttered. At a time when I had failed him most tragically, he reminded me that I was his son. . . . In the years that followed, he never once brought up that incident. He simply continued to love me for who I was and who I could be.

Our heavenly Father is like that: He's compassionate. He doesn't rub it in. He forgives.

---

6. Read Nehemiah's overview of God's dealings with Israel in Nehemiah 9:16-28. Though the Israelites rebelled again and again, and received just punishment for their sins, how did God respond to their sufferings?

7. How do you think He responds to you when you suffer as a result of your own sinfulness?

D Your Heavenly Father Is Holy

Once again it is Jesus who gives us insight about the Father. He taught us to pray: "Our Father in heaven, hallowed be Your name" (Matthew 6:9, NKJV).

Hallowed is a form of the word *holy*. It literally means "to set apart." God is set apart from sin, from impurity, from unrighteousness. And we "hallow" His name when we recognize His holiness, when we set Him apart in our lives as our Lord and King, when we honor and obey Him.

I learned something about holiness from my own father. Dad was a man of great integrity. I loved him, admired him, respected him, and wanted to be like him. To tell the truth, I even feared him a little.

About a year before he died I did something for which I was justly ashamed. Tearfully I confessed it to my dad. I guess I expected him to take off his belt and give me the spanking I knew I deserved. Instead he simply shook his head. His eyes reflected his sadness as he said softly, "Son, that's not the thing to do. . . ."

A hundred spankings wouldn't have hurt as much. I saw for the first time how my sin was an affront to his character, how what I did hurt him.

Your Father is a Holy God, so holy that the only way to satisfy His justice was for Jesus to die for your sins. But when you disobey, He doesn't start hurling lightning bolts at you. It's worse than that. You grieve Him, you hurt Him when you sin.

8. Why is it important for us to live holy lives (Leviticus 20:26)?

9. How did Isaiah respond when he got a glimpse of God's holiness (Isaiah 6:1-7)?

10. What did God do for Isaiah when he acknowledged his sin?

11. Why are believers, imperfect as we are, able to have fellowship with a holy God (1 Peter 3:18)?

D Your Heavenly Father Looks Like Jesus

Finally, remember that Jesus said, "Anyone who has seen me has seen the Father" (John 14:9).

You can believe in any kind of God you want. Paint Him angry. Color Him distant. Or go to the opposite extreme and sketch Him permissive. Decide that, like parents we all know, He just smiles while His kids run through life destroying things.

But remember one thing: Unless your heavenly Father looks and acts and reacts like Jesus, He's not real. The real Father, the One we must recognize and embrace, looks like the Jesus of Scripture.

What a help this can be! If you struggle to envision your Father's love or forgiveness, His strength or tenderness, take a good look at Jesus. Do you sometimes imagine your heavenly Father as an angry, distant God? Then see Jesus touching people, healing them, and crying over them.

When you look at Jesus, you'll see your heavenly Father, too. And as you envision His tender love toward a precious little child, know that it is the same affection He holds for you.

We've looked at four descriptions, or identification marks, of our heavenly Father. We've focused on who He is as a Father.

Now let's look at what He does. You can learn a lot about a person by following him around, watching what activities consume his life. So we need to see some of the activities of the Father to better recognize what He does in our lives.

Your Heavenly Father Gives to His Children

"Which of you, if his son asks for bread, will give him a stone? Or if he asks for a fish, will give him a snake? If you, then, though you are evil, know how to give good gifts to your children, how much more will your Father in heaven give good gifts to those who ask him!" (Matthew 7:9-11).

Jesus used a truth of human nature to tell us something about our heavenly Father. If evil men are often generous with their children, how much more is God the Father!

There are differences, though. Our heavenly Father always gives good gifts. The gifts that earthly fathers give may not be needed. They may even be wrong or harmful. But God always gives what is appropriate, necessary, and beneficial.

Giving is at the very heart of what our Father does. He is an expert at it. We are His creation, and He has given us life. He gave His Son, Jesus Christ, as the payment for our sins. When we become Christians, He gives us eternal life. In fact, every good thing we have is a gift from His hand (James 1:17).

In other words, it is your Father's nature to give. Align your will with His, accept His priorities, and His generosity will supply your every need (Matthew 6:33). Do you need forgiveness? Money? Perseverance? Emotional or physical strength? The Father gives everything that we need when we make His kingdom and righteousness our chief priorities.

---

12. a. Look again at James 1:17. In the space below, list as many good things in your life as you can—both tangible (like belongings or favorite places) and intangible (like relationships). Underline everything you listed that is a gift from God.

b. Were there some things on your list that you hadn't thought of before as gifts from God? Take a few moments to thank Him for His good gifts.

13. In the coming weeks, how can you remind yourself that all the good things in your life come from His hand?

D. Your Heavenly Father Disciplines His Children

Earthly fathers discipline as they think best. Often they make mistakes. But your heavenly Father never makes a mistake in discipline. His timing is perfect, His motives are pure, and His methods are never destructive. They are always beneficial.

What, exactly, is the discipline of God? The word *discipline* translated refers to training—training that sometimes incorporates punishment for disobedience, but always has future obedience as its goal. It is an act of love.

14. Fill in the blanks of the following verses, Hebrews 12:7, 10-11.

Endure hardship as discipline; God is treating you _____

_____. For what son is not disciplined by his father? . . . God

disciplines us _____. No discipline seems

pleasant at the time, but painful. Later on, however, it produces

_____ for those who have been trained by it.

15. God's discipline may come through circumstances—hard

times, suffering, even persecution. Or, it may come in other ways. Record your observations after reading the following verses:

- Ephesians 6:4

- Matthew 18:15-20

- Romans 13:1-7

D Whatever the means, discipline is always unpleasant (Hebrews 12:11). It is on the rough edges of life that we learn endurance, obedience, humility, compassion, and trust.

The ancient silversmith would heat crude silver ore in his crucible until the impurities rose to the top. Then he would skim off the slag and repeat the refining process. He knew he had achieved pure silver when, gazing into the molten metal, he could see his own reflection.

Our Father disciplines us in the crucible of trial and suffering, then skims away our impurities. His goal is to look into our lives and see the image of Jesus (Romans 8:29).

---

16. As you study three biblical men who were disciplined by God, fill in the information below:

a. 2 Samuel 11:1–12:19
- Person disciplined:

- Reason for discipline:

- Type of discipline:

- Result of discipline:

b. 2 Chronicles 33:1-16
  - Person disciplined:

  - Reason for discipline:

  - Type of discipline:

  - Result of discipline:

c. 2 Corinthians 12:7-10
  - Person disciplined:

  - Reason for discipline:

  - Type of discipline:

  - Result of discipline:

17. Pretend you are one of those characters and write a paragraph telling how you felt when the Lord disciplined you. Were you thankful for His discipline? Why?

18. Now take a look at your own life and write about a time when you experienced the Lord's discipline—either as a result of sin in your life or to build your character. What was the result?

19.   Are you experiencing the Lord's discipline now? If so, thank Him that He cares enough about you not to leave you where you are, but to push you toward deeper godliness.

D Your Heavenly Father Guides His Children

"I will lead them beside streams of water on a level path where they will not stumble" (Jeremiah 31:9).

God gave those words to Israel as a promise of return from exile, a reassurance of His love and protection. But the message rings true for all God's children everywhere.

20.   Look at God's promise in Jeremiah 29:11. What will be the result of God's plans for us?

21.   God says, "I will instruct you and teach you in the way you should go; I will counsel you and watch over you" (Psalm 32:8). What do God's promises of guidance say about what kind of Father He is?

D. Your Heavenly Father Never Forgets You

Our Father understands that many believers struggle to understand His loving fatherhood. Centuries ago He spoke to that very issue, reassuring His children of His love: "Can a mother forget the baby at her breast and have no compassion on the child she has borne? Though she may forget, I will not forget you! See, I have engraved you on the palms of my hands" (Isaiah 49:15-16).

Yes, your mother or father may have failed you. All parents fall short, and some fail tragically. But look into the Scriptures and see your heavenly Father for who He is and what He does. He seeks your fellowship, He offers to meet all your needs, He disciplines and guides in all the seasons of your life. And He never forgets you. He never rejects you when you come to Him.

How precious are you to your heavenly Father? Look! See the testimony of His love, engraved on the palms of His Son!

22. How does what you have learned in this study compare with your answers to question one of this session?

23. How might your relationship with God be different if you grasped and lived by this truth?

Parting Thought

God does not allow us to continue to reduce Him to a size and shape we can manage. He moves in our lives in ways that burst our categories and overwhelm our finiteness. When we realize He's bigger than anything we can get our minds around, we can begin to relax and enjoy Him.

—Paula Rinehart, from "Passages of Faith," Issue 75

4

Experiencing God's Love

 Before digging into any new material, spend some time reflecting on what you've learned so far about deepening your relationship with God. Review each of the sessions before answering the questions that correspond to it.

Session One: Keys to Intimacy

1. a Since beginning this study, how have you seen God pursuing a relationship with you? Have you seen any tangible signs of His love for you and desire for you to grow closer to Him?

   b. If so, how have you responded?

2. Think again about the following four aspects of becoming a friend of God. Next to each one, write a short statement about what you have learned or how you have grown in this

area since beginning this study. Or, describe how you would like to grow in this area and why.

■ Desire

■ Dependence

■ Abiding

■ Obedience

Session Two: Spending Time with God

3. a Look back at the two ideas you chose to incorporate into your quiet time in question twenty-one (page 30). How are you doing? What results have you seen from following these suggestions?

■ Results from Suggestion 1:

■ Results from Suggestion 2:

b. Is there anything else from Session Two that you would like to continue to remember or practice as you spend time with God?

Session Three: Knowing God

4. a. Review the following qualities of God described in the article:

- Your heavenly Father is perfect.
- Your heavenly Father is compassionate.
- Your heavenly Father is holy.
- Your heavenly Father looks like Jesus.

b. Underline the quality that means the most to you right now. Think about the week that lies ahead. How does knowing that God possesses this quality encourage you as you think of the challenges you will face?

5. a. Now review what your heavenly Father does for His children:

- Your heavenly Father gives to His children.
- Your heavenly Father disciplines His children.
- Your heavenly Father guides His children.
- Your heavenly Father never forgets you.

b. In the past week, how have you seen your heavenly Father working in your life? What has He done for you, His child?

c. Take a few minutes to thank Him for His involvement in your life.

6. What were the most significant insights you gained about God from Session Three?

⬛ Going Deeper

Until we begin to grasp the extent of God's love for us, we will probably not be motivated to seek Him. John wrote, "We love because he first loved us" (1 John 4:19). Let's stop now and take a look at God's love.

In the following excerpt from **"Our Father's Heart" by Phil Davis** (Issue 63), the author retells the story of the prodigal son, which he suggests could also be suitably titled "The Parable of the Loving Father." Jesus' story about a son who returns home in disgrace after squandering his inheritance gives us a moving picture of God's love for His children.

---

7. Read the excerpt below several times, putting yourself in the place of the returning son. Underline any phrases or sentences in the story that especially stand out to you.

⬛ A Father's Love

The father probably scanned the horizon daily, straining his eyes to spot a particular solitary silhouette coming across the heat waves rising from the arid land. And perhaps on more than one occasion, upon seeing a figure, he leaned forward and squinted his eyes to make out who it was. His heart might have beat a bit faster in anticipation—only to realize it wasn't his son, but one of the field hands or a stranger.

One day the father saw a figure in the distance, as he had many times before. . . . He stopped, wiping his brow, and slowly took a step forward, squinting into the distance. With the second step his heart beat faster. As only a parent can, he recognized his son's particular walk and stature.

Tense with hope, the father took a quick step or two and broke into a run, not taking his eyes off his son for fear it might be an illusion. He called a couple of servants to fall in behind him. He already knew his plan, for he had thought often of this moment. And he ran. It had been a long time since he had run this hard, but he hardly gave it a thought as his sandals flapped up clumps of dirt and dust clung to his disheveled robe.

By the time the son realized the man running toward him was his father, he might have frozen in his tracks, wondering if his father was enraged and would drive him off. But as he saw the bright eyes and toothy grin, he must have momentarily forgotten his rehearsed lines.

A lesser father would have waited for the son to arrive. A lesser father would have appeared a bit stoic and unmoved. Perhaps he would have not even lifted his eyes to meet the son, but instead would have shown his disapproval and hurt.

A lesser father would have outlined the conditions of the son's return instead of laying out the red carpet unconditionally. He would have waited for an apology before showing acceptance, and may not have warmed up until his son showed some real signs of change. A lesser father would have made it clear that the son had to prove himself worthy again.

But in the parable in Luke 15 we are not dealing with an average father. "While he was still a long way off, his father saw him and was filled with compassion for him; he ran to his son, threw his arms around him and kissed him" (verse 20).

---

8. What does this story tell you about God's love?

9. Look up the following verses about God's love. Spend several minutes meditating on what each truth means to you. Then respond to the applications below.

   a. 1 Chronicles 16:34
      ▪ Truth about God's love:

      ▪ What it means to me:

b. Psalm 32:10
- Truth about God's love:

- What it means to me:

c. Psalm 36:5
- Truth about God's love:

- What it means to me:

d. Psalm 63:3
- Truth about God's love:

- What it means to me:

e. Psalm 94:18
- Truth about God's love:

- What it means to me:

f. Isaiah 54:10
- Truth about God's love:

- What it means to me:

g. Romans 5:8
- Truth about God's love:

- What it means to me:

h. Romans 8:35-39
  - Truth about God's love:

  - What it means to me:

i. 1 John 3:1
  - Truth about God's love:

  - What it means to me:

10. Zephaniah 3:17 paints a vivid picture of God's love for His children. Write out this verse in your own words.

11. a. Review the verses you studied in questions nine and ten. Which one stands out to you the most?

  b. Why is that verse especially meaningful to you right now?

  c. You may want to memorize that verse so that you can contemplate it often in the coming weeks.

12. After reflecting on what you have studied in this session, draw a picture or diagram that represents God's love to you.

D The apostle John lived, traveled, and ministered with Jesus for more than two years. Jesus knew everything about him—including all his faults and shortcomings. Yet when he wrote his gospel, John referred to himself with one label: "the disciple whom Jesus loved" (John 13:23, 21:20). In the article entitled "The One Jesus Loves" (Issue 82), Brennan Manning observes, "If John were to be asked 'What is your primary identity, your most coherent sense of yourself?' he would not reply, 'I am a disciple, an apostle, an evangelist,' but 'I am the one Jesus loves.'"

13. The apostle Paul suggests two other labels under which all believers can think of themselves. What are they?

- Ephesians 5:1, NASB

- 1 Thessalonians 1:4, NASB

14. What if your driver's license, the nameplate at your office, your checkbook, and so on, all bore the name "child of God" or "beloved by God" instead of your given name? What if you introduced yourself by saying, "Hello, I'm beloved by God"? How might that change your outlook on life?

15. How can you remind yourself throughout this next week that you are "beloved by God"?

16. Paul prayed that the Ephesians would have the power "to grasp how wide and long and high and deep is the love of Christ, and to know this love that surpasses knowledge—that [they] may be filled to the measure of all the fullness of God" (Ephesians 3:17-19). Is there someone who could pray this verse for you? Write his or her name below and ask him or her this week to pray that you would experience God's love in increasing measure.

17. Do you know someone else who needs a firmer grasp on God's love for him or her? Pray Ephesians 3:17-19 for him or her this week.

Parting Thought

Those times when we feel most keenly our unworthiness to enter the presence of God are times when we gain the most insight into God's mercy.

—Mike Treneer, from "The Mercy of God," Issue 36

5

Hindrances to Knowing God

The following article, entitled **"What's Stopping You?" by Jill Briscoe** (excerpted from Issue 85), explores the various hindrances that keep us from knowing God more deeply. As you read, highlight any thoughts or suggestions that stand out to you.

Awareness Is Not Knowing

On a typically beautiful British autumn day in 1969, my husband came cheerily into the house and announced, "Well kids, we're moving to America!" My heart pumped furiously. What would it all mean for the Briscoe family?

"I know about America," our son David offered. "We studied it in school this year."

It was true David did know a little about America. But awareness wasn't knowing. In the months ahead, Stuart (who was already traveling in the United States) would send us photographs or make wonderfully descriptive audiotapes, adding details to our knowledge. The more we gained information, the more we began to get excited. Dad brought home baseball hats, magnets for my fridge, and a Barbie doll for Judy. But the information we gained and even our warm feelings did not constitute a true knowing.

Knowing God, like knowing America, is much more than awareness, information, or emotional stirrings. Knowing is being there. Too many of us never get beyond a textbook acquaintance with God. We remain across the sea, content to base our knowledge mainly on what others describe to us. What keeps us from truly experiencing God?

D The Bane of Busyness

There is some busyness that is blessed busyness and there is some that is a bane. Some of us are busy doing important things, and some of us are busy doing unimportant things, and some of us are just busy being busy! How busy is too busy? Who will tell me? God will! I need to learn the art of leaving things undone.

Whether it be housework, raising children, church work, or work in the secular marketplace, there is no end to the jobs that need to be done. Yet I've found that even though there is a world to be won, God expects me to attend first to the mission field at my own two feet. There are millions of hungry people to be fed, but God only expects me to offer up the fish and bread in my own lunch basket. There are children to be trained, but I am responsible first and foremost to raise my own. And there are certainly lots of Christians to be discipled, counseled, and helped, but I didn't save them, and I don't have to keep them! It's all a matter of the art of leaving things undone.

Jesus knew how to do that. One day He said to His heavenly Father, "I have finished the work which You have given Me to do" (John 17:4, NKJV), and went home to heaven at the age of 33. Think about that. Think of all the lepers He left behind; all the hungry, maimed, blind, and demon-possessed who stayed hungry, maimed, blind, and demon-possessed. You may be tempted to ask, How could He have finished the work that needed to be done? Oh, but it doesn't say He finished the work that needed to be done—it says He finished the work God gave Him to do. And that's why it's important to learn the secret of pleasing God! Jesus said, "I always do what pleases him" (John 8:29).

---

1. In the space below, list everything that is "on your plate," keeping you busy this week, both inside and outside the home.

2. How do you feel about leaving things undone? Check the response that is closest to yours:

☐ I feel anxious when things are left undone.
☐ I can relax when things are left undone—I can't do it all!
☐ Other:

3. Sometimes we overcommit ourselves because we want to please others. Have you ever done something to please someone else without praying about it? Check all the people you've been tempted to please in this way.

☐ Employer   ☐ Spouse
☐ Children   ☐ Friends
☐ Parents   ☐ People at church
☐ Other:

4. Choose one such instance and write what happened as a result.

5. a. According to Galatians 1:10, what can you *not* be if you are striving to please people?

   b. Why is this true?

6. What do the following verses indicate about ensuring that we're busy with the right things?

    ▪ Psalm 32:8

    ▪ James 1:5-6

    ▪ Proverbs 12:15, 15:22

D When we please Him by getting on with the work He gave us to do, we will find that we stay closer to Him. We won't get so busy we get dizzy with doing. We'll be able to come to terms with the dying and the crying. We'll pray more effectively that God would send out other laborers to do the work He's given them to do, while we busy ourselves with our own blessed business. And most important, we won't rob others of the joy of hearing their "well done" at the end of the day.

Maybe we should examine our hearts in this matter and make sure we can say, "I always do those things that please Him." If we can strive to do that, we will have learned the art of leaving things undone and find ourselves only doing *our part*.

---

7. Read the story of Mary and Martha in Luke 10:38-42. Describe a time when you felt like Martha.

8. What would "choosing what is better" have looked like in the situation you described? How might it have helped you?

9.   What do you think Jesus is saying to you through this passage?

10. Is busyness keeping you from spending enough time with God to get to know Him better? Review your "busy list" from question one (page 54). Pray about each item. Is God leading you to let go of something so that you'll have time for the "one thing" that's most important?

The Problem of Pettiness

What stops us from staying in touch with God? Busyness, and often pettiness. All of us can fall into the pettiness trap.

What is pettiness? Pettiness bothers our heads with whether we are too hot or too cool as we sit in a cushy church sanctuary; whether someone took our spot in the church parking lot; or whether anyone noticed or acknowledged our latest contribution. Pettiness bites and devours our brothers and sisters in the Lord. It stops us from ever hearing the voice of God through the pastor, who, pettiness insists, is either "too shallow" or "too deep."

11. Do you ever come away from a church service or small group more focused on the shortcomings of the leaders or the people there than on what God was saying to you through it? How could this critical spirit keep you from knowing God?

12. Think about what Jesus said to those who were critical of
    others (Matthew 7:1-5). Describe how applying the truths in
    these verses could help you avoid criticizing spiritual leaders.

    ▪ Verses 1-2:

    ▪ Verses 3-5:

D I constantly ask the Lord to keep me from having a mini-
mind-set. From thinking small, easy, below average. When I'm
maxi-minded instead of petty, I try to make a difference where I
live—to be salt, to arrest corruption, and to be light in a dark place.
    One day Jesus listened to His disciples arguing about lunch!
"Open your eyes," He advised them. "Look at the fields! They are
ripe for harvest" (John 4:35). If we have our eyes fixed on the loaf
of bread in our hands, we'll never see the One who grew the grain
in the first place. When multitudes of hungry people need to be
fed, we may find ourselves arguing which bread is best—whole
wheat or white! The Lord needs to deliver us from being fascinated
and captivated by our lunch. May the needs of a spiritually starved
world lift us above the pettiness that so easily besets us.

---

13. Jesus had a clear vision for why He was on earth. What were
    His purposes in being here?

    ▪ Mark 1:38, John 18:37

    ▪ John 6:38

    ▪ John 10:10, 12:27

14. As we follow in Jesus' footsteps, on what should we focus our thoughts, our energies, and our very lives?

The Lure of Laziness

What keeps me from growing close to God? Busyness, pettiness, and, of course, laziness will do it. Sheer unadulterated laziness. We simply can't be bothered to be bothered. Laziness is a willful decision not to go to good extremes.

Laziness yawns when he hears a talk on laziness. He tunes out easily, too lazy to listen to the application. He's too lazy to concentrate on anything spiritually stretching at all, preferring drama to doctrine and music to mastering the Scriptures. He wants to be entertained, not educated. If electives are offered at church, he carefully selects ones titled "How to Find Rest for Your Soul" or "How to Pray Effectively in Five Minutes Flat." He always arranges to work late at the office during a missions festival.

15. How do the following verses about laziness apply to your spiritual life?

- Proverbs 13:4

- Proverbs 20:4

- Proverbs 22:13

16. Laziness can affect your relationship with God. Describe how it could hinder your growth in the following areas:

■ Quiet time

■ Bible study

■ Fellowship

■ Witnessing

■ Service

D Being naturally lazy at heart (the flesh is weak, remember), I find I need to make some commitments to real live people and not just to God. I find someone somewhere to teach. Just to make an appointment once or twice a week with someone not quite as far along in the faith as you are (and you can always find one of those) will do it. This means I have to be in the Word so I can pass it along. I will need to have something new to say each time we meet. Laziness doesn't like this, but God does.

I also fight laziness by choosing a day (mine is Sunday) when I promise the Lord and myself I'll jot a note, scribble a letter, make a phone call, or send something to encourage or build up someone, somewhere, somehow. Having a certain day of the week helps me to avoid laziness' temptations to procrastinate.

I've noticed laziness' favorite day of the week is "tomorrow." Laziness negates the importance of today. Yet we all need to live today as if we had no other days, knowing full well tomorrow may never come.

17. In which of the five areas in question sixteen are you most prone to be lazy?

18. Take a look at your answer to question seventeen. What could you do to avoid laziness in this area?

D The Fear of the Cost

Busyness, pettiness, laziness . . . all these can keep us at an arm's length from God. But perhaps the biggest obstacle to knowing God is that we fear the cost of it all.

Jesus called Peter to follow Him. For Peter this call was to leave everything and follow Jesus.

What did that mean for Peter and his family? It meant leaving his business and security, his home and environment, his trade, his independence. Peter must have feared the cost. But because he experienced the power of Christ in the miraculous catch of fish, he fell at the Lord's feet. His heart was captured and his mind convinced that Jesus was Lord. When he heard the Lord's words, "Don't be afraid; from now on you will catch men," he beached his boat and began an experience of "knowing" God he could never have had without paying a price.

19. Suppose Jesus asked you to leave everything in order to preach the gospel in a remote village in a distant country. What in your present life would be hardest for you to give up?

☐ Financial security   ☐ My career
☐ My comfort   ☐ My family's safety and comfort
☐ My possessions   ☐ Media or entertainment
☐ Others' respect   ☐ Friends and relatives nearby
☐ Other:

20. Are any of these things hindering your relationship with God now? If so, how?

21. Jesus said, "Whoever finds his life will lose it, and whoever loses his life for my sake will find it" (Matthew 10:39). What do you think it means to lose your life for Jesus' sake?

22. How does that prospect make you feel?

D There is a cost to knowing God. There has to be. Because the more you know, the more you long for others to know too. And that longing could well take you not only across the street, but perhaps even around the world!

When the church invited us to leave England and move to the United States, they asked us to "beach our boats." We came with the clothes we needed and that was all. Up to then we had known God as provider; now we were invited to know Him in a new and deeper way. But there was a cost. All of us were afraid, but we followed Him. Sometimes I long for England, my "Galilee"—the quiet meadows and serene peaks and golden daffodils. But that's part of the price. The cost of obedience, however, is totally outweighed by the depth and joy of a new "knowing" of the Lord.

23. In John 12:24-25, what two rewards does Jesus promise to those who let go of their lives?

D Slaying the Sinful Self

So what in the end can keep me from coming closer to God? I can! In the final analysis it is that sinful self—the flesh—I have been describing. My fallen nature knows how to be hostile to God. The main problem is that I don't want to be like Jesus, I want to be like me. That's the essence of the flesh. Self is all for getting, not giving; living, not dying; controlling, not releasing. What stops Jill Briscoe from staying near to God? Jill Briscoe! And it never gets any easier.

Paul talks about this in Romans 7:21-24. The battle that rages within will rage until it's over and we are home in heaven. We have two natures warring inside of us. It's a bit like the English bird that lays its eggs in its nest and sets about hatching them. Along comes the cuckoo bird (a lazy fellow). It can't bother building its own nest, so it plops its egg in the nest already occupied. Two natures in one nest! The diligent bird hatches all the eggs. Now the cuckoo baby—bigger, and nasty—grows and grows, snatching the food and taking over. Eventually, the cuckoo tips the rightful little owners out and reigns supreme. What a picture of the fleshly nature! The nature we feed will control life in the nest!

So whether it's busyness, pettiness, laziness, or the cost, it's our innate selfishness that needs to be hammered to the cross of Christ moment by moment and day by day. Who will take the hammer and fasten me to the cross? Someone already has! For as in Christ all died, so in Him all will be made alive. There it is! I can reckon myself dead indeed unto sin but alive unto God. That's a mind-set that begins in my head, then captures my heart, and finally sets my feet dancing with delight. I find that dying to self is not such a dreadful idea after all, for such a death releases me into the power and pleasure of His daily presence and delivers me from me.

So what keeps us from knowing and experiencing God in a more meaningful way? Whatever it is, it's not worth a wasted life.

24. Four things can keep us from intimacy with God: busyness, pettiness, laziness, and the cost. Which of these is the greatest hindrance to deepening your relationship with God?

25. How does this hinder you from loving God "with all your heart and with all your soul and with all your mind and with all your strength" (Mark 12:30)?

26. How could you begin to break down this barrier to your relationship with God? What part will God, other believers, and your own choices play in this process?

Parting Thought

Do we find ourselves a little hesitant to unreservedly commit an area of our life to the Lord for fear of what He might require? Then we haven't seen Him in His beauty yet.

—Joyce Turner, from "At Home with God," Issue 1

6

Listening to God

Do you ever wish you could talk to God face-to-face? Do you have a list of questions you'd like to ask Him? Wouldn't it be great if He would just tell you every morning what He wants you to do that day—if He would help you make the right decisions and avoid costly mistakes?

God does give us the answers to many of our questions—today! His guidance is available when we need it. He does warn us about danger ahead. But too often, we don't know how to listen. In this session, we'll look at how we can improve our ability to hear God's voice.

1. a. If you could hear God speaking directly to you right now, what would you want Him to talk to you about?

   ☐ A decision
   ☐ A problem
   ☐ An assurance of His love for me
   ☐ Other:

   b. What questions would you like to ask God?

The following article, entitled **"Hearing God's Voice" by Martha Thatcher** (excerpted from Issue 37), explores the various ways we listen to God. As you read, underline any thoughts that stand out to you. Then move on to the questions and exercises.

When the Master Calls

My childhood home was around the corner from a tree-lined field. Many evenings I took my dog Skippy there for an after-supper romp.

Other dog owners had discovered the same field. When it was time to leave, we all chased our pets around the field in an often frustrating effort to hook leash to collar.

There was one man, however, whose relationship with his dog stood out in sharp contrast to the rest of us. When the man was ready to go, he stayed where he was and said, "Come." We would all watch in envy and astonishment as one large brown head suddenly lifted from the noisy pack and turned to find the voice. Then this dog would run to his master's side, where he'd sit, panting with the excitement of responding to his master's command.

Years later, this experience helped me to glimpse some insights into how a person learns to hear the voice of God. One dog in that pack had learned to hear and respond to his master's voice. His training had taken place in private, without the distractions of the noisy field. The result was that even amid the confusion of play, that dog's ear was tuned to his master's word. He immediately singled out and obeyed his owner's command to "come."

Jesus used a word picture of a similar response when He said, "My sheep listen to my voice; I know them, and they follow me" (John 10:27). What is involved in hearing the voice of our Master?

The Bible: God's Word to Us

The Bible is the active voice of our living God, communicating Himself to us. His person, His character, His ways of dealing with people, and His purposes all remain eternally unchanged and unchanging, revealed in His Word. Not only has God spoken, He still speaks. He speaks to you and to me today about Himself, about His truth, and about us, His creation. And what He says is indispensable to our lives: "The words I have spoken to you are spirit and they are life" (John 6:63).

Our interaction with God in His Word is our private training to recognize and listen to His voice. As we read, hear, study, memorize, and think about God's Word, our Shepherd's voice becomes more distinct to us, more easily discerned in the din of life.

2. Read about Jesus' temptation in the wilderness (Matthew 4:1-11). How did Jesus combat Satan's tempting suggestions?

3. Has your knowledge of Scripture ever helped you hear God's voice in a difficult or confusing situation? Describe what happened.

How much time do we spend reading and studying God's Word? Do we dig around in it only to find answers to our current questions, or are we opening ourselves to the Scriptures often and regularly? Mundane questions, perhaps. But let's not be too quick to dismiss them. Often what we wish were true is quite different from what is true.

4. Think back over the last week. How much time did you spend reading, studying, memorizing, and praying over the Bible?

5. If you wanted to increase the amount of time you spend in God's Word, what changes could you make next week to make that possible?

D But even time spent listening is not in itself any guarantee of hearing the voice of God. In the third chapter of his gospel, Mark records that some teachers of the law came from Jerusalem to observe Jesus and hear what He had to say. The primary responsibility of these men was to examine and copy the Scriptures. After listening and watching, they accused Jesus of being demon-possessed. The very ones who spent most of their time in the Scriptures were totally unable to recognize God's voice when they heard it. Study time in itself guarantees nothing.

When we come to God in His Word, we must bring believing hearts. We are listening to the living communication of a powerful and loving God with His needy people. Could His words possibly be insensitive to who we are and where we are?

When we believe that God lovingly seeks our best and that He is vastly more sensitive to us than we are to ourselves, we will seek to hear Him. When we doubt God's intentions, His intimate caring, or His ability to speak directly to us and work powerfully in our lives, we may go through the motions of Bible reading, but we won't be listening expectantly to God. We will relegate God's thoughts to the "spiritual" part of our lives, while we live out our days in the remaining realms.

6. The author says that if we doubt that God truly cares about us, we won't be motivated to listen to Him. Why is this true?

7. a. Romans 8:28 says that "in all things God works for the good of those who love him, who have been called according to his purpose." According to verse 29, what is the "good," the purpose toward which God is directing the events of our lives?

b. Why, then, is it especially important to listen to Him when we go through difficult times in our lives?

D When I hear what God is saying to me, it will most likely require that I change and grow. If my status quo is very comfortable, I will by all means resist change! But if I trust God for His loving character and His good intentions toward me, I will open myself to change, believing that He knows better than I do what is needed in my life.

The book of Proverbs encourages us to hone our availability and attitude into an intense pursuit of what God has to say in His Word. We are not merely to be passively open and willing when God speaks, but we are to aggressively seek to know God's thoughts more and more. Solomon uses forceful words to describe the intensity of the seeking listener:

> *If you call out for insight*
> *and cry aloud for understanding,*
> *and if you look for it as for silver*
> *and search for it as for hidden treasure,*
> *then you will understand the fear of the LORD*
> *and find the knowledge of God. (Proverbs 2:3-5)*

8. a. Underline the active verbs in the first four lines of the verses above. Describe the attitude we need to have as we read and study God's Word.

   b. What does this passage promise to those who diligently seek God?

D **Training Our Ears**

Perhaps you have had the experience, as I have, of wishing the words on the page would suddenly come alive. Yet you've once again been discouraged to find that despite your earnest intention, they remained simply printed words.

Why do God's words sometimes seem lifeless? Let's assume we have dealt with any sin of which we are conscious (for sin surely deafens us more effectively than anything else), made ourselves available to God in His Word, and come to Him trusting His person. Then we must give our attention to the focus of our listening: What are we listening for when we open our Bibles?

See if you recognize any of these responses: "I'm not getting anything out of my quiet time (Bible study) lately"; "God isn't making Himself clear about what I should do"; "I keep asking God about my problem, but He hasn't given me any answers"; "I wish the Bible seemed more relevant to me—it's so dry and obscure most of the time."

---

9. Underline any of the responses in the preceding paragraph that sound like something you've said or thought recently.

D Not one of these concerns is wrong, but all reflect a deviation of focus. These concerns are issue-centered, not God-centered. They focus on what God is saying, without a prior focus on God Himself. Issue-centered listening is a perilous endeavor. By nature it is both selective and pressured. Often what results from such listening is a misuse of Scripture, an attempt to use one verse as a simple answer to a complex situation or to justify a preference with Bible quotes.

This kind of listening commits the sin of treating God as a means, not an end. With such a frame of mind, whether we realize it or not, we are using God to try to get what we think we need. Instead, God calls us to listen to Him, to seek His face; He will take care of our needs.

And so, as we open the Word, our hearts should cry out with David, "Your face, Lord, I will seek" (Psalm 27:8). We can devise questions that will help keep this focus: What is revealed about God in these verses? What do I see of God's character or His work among men in this passage? How is God responding in this event or circumstance?

10. Psalm 63 gives us a picture of a heart that aches for God Himself. As you look at each phrase, jot down what it reveals about God's character, how He responds to our circumstances, or how we should respond to Him.

- O God, you are my God, earnestly I seek you.

- My soul thirsts for you, my body longs for you, in a dry and weary land where there is no water.

- I have seen you in the sanctuary and beheld your power and your glory.

- Because your love is better than life, my lips will glorify you.

- I will praise you as long as I live, and in your name I will lift up my hands.

- My soul will be satisfied as with the richest of foods.

- With singing lips my mouth will praise you.

- On my bed I remember you; I think of you through the watches of the night.

- Because you are my help, I sing in the shadow of your wings.

- My soul clings to you; your right hand upholds me.

When we seek God in His Word, we will find ourselves hearing Him. We will know Him better and better and, in that context, the truths He reveals will become profoundly meaningful to our everyday existence.

Hearing His Voice

There are basically two arenas in which we listen to God. One is the quiet, private times with God in His Word. The second arena in which we hear the voice of God is out in our "field." Only a small proportion of our time is spent in private involvement with God in His Word. Yet God is everywhere, seeking always and without ceasing to communicate Himself to us. He will bring to mind the truths He has shared with us in private, and through circumstances and people we will hear the echo of the voice we hear directly in His Word.

Much of what happens in our lives is God's nonverbal communication with us. Do we find ourselves thrown about by a series of unexpected events? Perhaps God is saying, "Trust me." Are we hurt and disappointed that plans or relationships haven't materialized in the way we had hoped? It may be that God is telling us that He alone is our security. Have we watched people's lives turn around as they chose to obey God? Maybe He is helping us observe how pleased He is with obedience. The writer of Proverbs learned such lessons from God by observation: "I applied my heart to what I observed and learned a lesson from what I saw" (Proverbs 24:32).

11. Think about the author's statement "Much of what happens in our lives is God's nonverbal communication with us." Describe a time when God seemed to be clearly speaking to you through people or events.

12. Now think about the events of the last week. What might God have been saying to you through the ups or downs of the last seven days?

13. Read the story of David and Abigail in 1 Samuel 25. What did David recognize as the source of Abigail's message (verse 32)?

Abigail gave King David a stern but gracious warning. David recognized the voice of his Master in Abigail's message because he knew God. Even during his sword-brandishing, angry, and determined journey to attack Nabal and his men, David heard when God spoke.

Any voice we recognize as God's in the field of life must be the same voice we hear in the Bible. If we haven't cultivated our familiarity with God's powerfully comforting voice behind closed doors, we are in danger of mistaking many field voices as God's. Much of what we hear, even in our Christian circles, sounds good, but it does not come from God. Or, even though it reflects God's truth, it may not be God's timely instruction for us. We can tie ourselves in knots when, because we do not hear God, we try to follow all the right sounding voices, all the ones that claim God's direction.

---

14. Read the story of "the man of God" in 1 Kings 13:1-25. What does it tell you about listening to godly people instead of to what God has told you?

15. Have you ever followed teaching or advice from well-meaning Christians, and realized later that what they said was not from God? What do the following passages have to say about avoiding this error?

▪ Proverbs 15:22

▪ Acts 17:11

▪ 1 John 4:1

The Purpose of Listening

God doesn't speak just to be heard. Nor does He reveal Himself only to be observed. He speaks, He reveals Himself, and He trains us to listen so that we can live out His words and reflect His person. Our hearing is meant to culminate in obedience. This is the nature of the Shepherd-sheep relationship to which Jesus was referring when He spoke of our recognizing His voice.

Sheep are trained to know only one shepherd and his call. Without his direction they are hapless and helpless, bringing trouble and confusion upon themselves and any other sheep who might follow them. But when they hear and follow the voice of their shepherd, they are safe, nourished, and secure. How sheeplike we are! Let's commit ourselves to listening to our Shepherd and following His voice. As we train ourselves to hear and obey His voice, we'll rejoice in the knowledge of His loving presence.

Parting Thought
The treasure to be found in Scripture is not a new thing that God says to me, but rather what He has been saying through Scripture ever since it was written.
—Keith White, from "Blueprint for Bible Study," Issue 6

7

Keeping the Passion Alive

1. Check off any of the following statements that apply to you.

    ☐ The gospels seem like reruns.
    ☐ My mind and mouth switch to automatic pilot during hymns and praise choruses.
    ☐ The last time God answered my prayers is a distant memory.
    ☐ I feel guilty when people describe what they learned in their quiet time—and hope they don't ask about mine.
    ☐ Where did the joy go?
    ☐ I don't go to Sunday school—"Been there, done that."
    ☐ I read my Bible and pray because I am supposed to. Period.
    ☐ I'm more excited about my favorite team than about Jesus.
    ☐ It doesn't seem like I'm growing spiritually anymore.
    ☐ I'm not really sure I love God, or that He loves me.
    ☐ I'm bored with the routine of my spiritual life.
    ☐ Those smiling, happy Christians get on my nerves.

If you checked more than three of the statements above, chances are that your spiritual flame is burning low. Even one check mark can be a warning signal that something is wrong.

Everyone who walks with God goes through times when God seems far away, when passion for Him dims to barely a flicker. If that's where you are, how can you fan the flame of your love for God? If your love for God is still strong, how can you make sure it stays that way? The following article by **Steven J. Lawson** (excerpted from "**Falling in Love Again**," Issue 84) addresses this issue. As you read the article, highlight those ideas that stand out to you, then go on to the questions and exercises.

Our Love Story

Ours is the greatest love story ever known. The King of kings courted us, lowly peasants that we were, and pursued us to become His royal bride.

At first, our love showed that we were the definition of romance. Bible study was so life changing. Prayer was so heart lifting. Worship was so earthshaking. We savored every moment in His presence.

But, as in any relationship, our love for Christ is subject to fluctuation. Sometimes there is a serious waning of our intensity. Sometimes our passion for the Lord grows stale. Mechanical. Routine. And we begin to take Him for granted.

Sure, we are still the bride of Jesus Christ. And, legally, we are still married. But we are merely coexisting. We share the same heart, but the relationship has grown cold. Distant.

Sadly, such a separation happened to some believers in the first century.

---

2.   At what stage of the "romance" are you right now?

☐ The thrill of romance—madly in love with Jesus
☐ The honeymoon is over—still in love, but lacking the passion that once was there
☐ The thrill is gone—going through the motions without the emotions
☐ Other:

An Extraordinary Church

Ephesus was one extraordinary church! We are not surprised that Jesus began this letter by commending the believers there.

"I know your deeds and your toil and perseverance, and that you cannot endure evil men, and you put to the test those who call

themselves apostles, and they are not, and you found them to be false; and you have perseverance and have endured for My name's sake, and have not grown weary." (Revelation 2:2-3, NASB)

Christianity was no spectator sport here. They didn't come to church to be entertained. They were actively involved in the work of ministry. Serving. Doing. Toiling. Giving. Going. When they took on a task, they stuck with it until the job was finished. They set a high moral standard and chose not to tolerate sin in the camp. When traveling teachers came to Ephesus, their doctrine was put to the test before they could get into the pulpit. While living in the hub of paganism, they held tenaciously to their witness for Christ. Even their motives were right. They endured for Christ's name's sake, not their own.

What could possibly have been wrong with a church like this? Plenty. They had everything but the main thing.

The Fatal Flaw

Abruptly, Jesus changed the tone of this letter. The Master put His finger on the one glaring deficiency in this church that threatened to ruin everything else. He had to address a fatal flaw—a deadly sin—so serious that it endangered the church's very existence. "But I have this against you, that you have left your first love" (Revelation 2:4, NASB).

Something was missing. This church had left its first love. Amid the Ephesians' many ministries and their tenacious stand for the truth, their love for Christ had grown cold.

First love is the fervent, passionate, red-hot love of a newly wedded couple. It pictures the romantic love that a couple feels when they first start dating. A chemistry happens. A mystical attraction occurs. Two lives fall in love, get married, and become one.

But somewhere in the daily routine of marriage, the honeymoon ceases. The children come. The career takes off. The business expands. The activities increase. The stresses multiply. And suddenly two people wake up complete strangers.

This slow leak is what left Ephesus flat. Their devoted love for Christ had cooled off. Their ministry had become mechanical. Their relationship had become routine. They were still coming to church. They were still serving. And they were still believing rightly. But their hearts were no longer in it.

Wives, imagine that your husband came home and said, "I don't love you anymore. But nothing will change. I'll still earn a living and pay the bills. We'll still sit together and sleep together. I'll still father our children. I just don't love you anymore." Would that be good enough for you?

No way. You would be devastated. Yet, we say that to the Lord. "Jesus, I don't love You like I once did. But I'll still come to church. I'll still serve You. I'll still witness for You. I just don't love You."

That's not good enough for Jesus either! He wants a relationship, not a performance. Jesus told them that their hearts had grown cold toward Him. He said, "You have left your first love."

---

3. Reflect on the analogy the author uses of the husband who no longer loves his wife. If you were that wife, how would you feel?

4. What does this analogy tell you about how God must feel when your passion for Him grows cold?

5. In the book of Revelation, Jesus rebuked another group of believers whose passion for Him had faded. What did He say to the church at Laodicea (Revelation 3:15-16)?

6. Which one of the following do you think is true? Check one, then explain your answer below.

    ☐ Everyone gets a little lazy spiritually from time to time. It's no big deal.
    ☐ God considers it a very serious matter when our love for Him cools.

D Jesus said that the greatest commandment is to love God (Matthew 22:37-39). We must love Him with all of our heart, soul, mind, and strength. Love for Christ must fill every inch of our being. Without love for Him, we are just "a noisy gong or a clanging cymbal" (1 Corinthians 13:1, NASB). Our hearts must pulsate with a blazing, passionate, vibrant love for Christ or we are nothing.

If we fail to love Him, we disobey the greatest commandment. It doesn't matter what else we obey if we fail to keep the highest commandment. Leaving our first love is the greatest sin.

---

7. Do you agree with the statement "Our hearts must pulsate with a blazing, passionate, vibrant love for Christ or we are nothing"? Why or why not?

8. Do you agree with the statement "Leaving our first love is the greatest sin"? Why or why not?

D. Falling in Love Again

With a yearning heart, Jesus pleaded with the Ephesian church. With arms wide open, He prescribed the steps that lead back to the honeymoon stage. Here is how we again draw close to Him. Here's how to fall back in love with Christ. Jesus said:

"Remember therefore from where you have fallen, and repent and do the deeds you did at first; or else I am coming to you, and will remove your lampstand out of its place—unless you repent." (Revelation 2:5, NASB)

Step One: Remember

First, Jesus said, "Remember therefore from where you have fallen." In other words, remember when you first came to faith in Christ. Replay that initial excitement.

Can you remember when you first fell in love with Christ? I can. After I graduated from college, I attended a dynamic church in Memphis, Tennessee. Every time they opened the church's doors, I was sitting in the middle of the front row. Everything the preacher had to say was for me. I shed tears when the choir sang. The Holy Spirit tugged on my heart when people were saved.

For some of us, such a time was only three months ago. For others, it was three years ago. For others, ten years ago.

The road back to Christ begins by first remembering. Remember the joy that was yours with Him. Get a good look at when you were on fire for Him.

That's where revival begins—remember!

---

9. a. Think back to the time in your life when you were most in love with the Lord. What was it about Him that affected you so deeply? What made you love Him?

b. Describe how you felt about Him at that time.

c. What Scriptures meant the most to you during that period?

d. What would you most like to recapture about that time in your life?

D Step Two: Repent

Second, Jesus said, "Repent." After you remember, repent! Repentance means to change the direction of your life. It is a change of heart. A change of mind. A change of will. It is a turning around and coming back to Christ.

The fact is, something or someone has replaced your first love. It's not that you don't have a first love anymore. It's that you have a new first love. Anything or anyone that you are more excited about than you are about Christ is your new first love.

Repent! Get on your knees and confess your spiritual apathy. Turn your cold heart back to Christ. As a decisive act of your will, choose to change your heart.

Say, "God, my heart has been distant from You. I've been far away from You. Lord, I want to change. Jesus, I'm turning my life around right now. Right now, I'm rededicating my life afresh to You. God, I want the passion for You back in my life."

10. As you search your heart, do you discover that you have a new first love? If so, what is it?
    □ Your job   □ A relationship
    □ Your family   □ Your education
    □ Your house   □ A hobby
    □ Your ministry   □ Sports
    □ Other:

11. The prophet Jeremiah said of God's children who refused to repent, "Each pursues his own course like a horse charging into battle" (Jeremiah 8:6). Why is this an apt analogy for those who fail to repent?

12. According to Acts 3:19, what happens after we repent?

13. Jesus warned the religious leaders, "Produce fruit in keeping with repentance" (Matthew 3:8). In other words, true repentance leads to a change in your actions. If you have felt the need to repent, what will you do differently now?

D Step Three: Repeat

Third, Jesus said, "Do the deeds you did at first." In other words, "Get back to the basics." What are these first deeds?

Simply put, these first deeds are what the early believers did when they were first saved and added to the church. They were "continually devoting themselves to the apostles' teaching and to fellowship, to the breaking of bread and to prayer" (Acts 2:42, NASB).

They studied the apostles' teaching. Biblical truth is essential to the health of every believer. It is the Word of God that stimulates our hearts to love Christ.

They maintained close fellowship. They were continually sharing and encouraging one another. Bearing one another's burdens. Comforting one another's hearts.

They came together to break bread. The early church worshiped Christ by regularly taking the Lord's Supper together. Communion with the living Christ kept their hearts aflame. The Lord's Table cultivated reverence, gratitude, purity, and the anticipation of Christ's return.

They devoted themselves to prayer. These early disciples spent much time on their knees. Kneeling in God's presence was as necessary as breathing. Daily, they enjoyed intimate fellowship with Him. Prayer transforms God's truth into personal devotion to Christ. It keeps us fervent for our first love.

---

14. How have you seen these "first deeds" affect your love for Christ? Respond to the following areas.

a. Bible Teaching
- How it stimulates my love for Christ:

- How neglecting it affects my love for Christ:

b. Fellowship
- How it stimulates my love for Christ:

- How neglecting it affects my love for Christ:

c. The Lord's Supper
- How it stimulates my love for Christ:

- How neglecting it affects my love for Christ:

d. Prayer
- How it stimulates my love for Christ:

- How neglecting it affects my love for Christs:

D A Radical Step

I had become so busy serving the church and so preoccupied with our kids that I was neglecting my wife, Anne. I would rise early, sprint to the office, study for sermons, return phone calls, dash home, play with our kids, eat dinner, help with homework, put children to bed, then collapse. Day after day. Week after week. Month after month.

I felt too exhausted to talk to my wife. Even when I tried to talk to her, I couldn't. The phone would ring. The kids would cry. The church would call. Or I was too tired.

Has your relationship with Christ become too busy? Are you too hurried to spend time with Him? Are you too active? Too distant? Too cold? Too impersonal?

Then take decisive steps right now. Remember how it was when you first met Christ. Repent of your cold-heartedness. Repeat the basics—Bible study, fellowship, worship, and prayer. Determine to be alone with Christ. He's waiting to be alone with you.

15. What would you do if you had an extended period of uninterrupted time with the Lord—just the two of you? Get out your calendar and schedule a "date" with the Lord.

Parting Thought
If we cannot recognize the value of simply being alone with God, as the beloved, without doing anything, we gouge the heart out of Christianity.
—Brennan Manning, from "Grabbing Aholt of God," Issue 80

8

Going On with God

Before digging into any new material, let's look back at what you've learned in the last few chapters about deepening your relationship with God. Review each of the sessions before answering the questions that correspond to it.

Session Five: Hindrances to Knowing God

1. Jill Briscoe writes about four things that can keep us from knowing God: busyness, pettiness, laziness, and the cost. Reflect over the weeks since you studied Session Five. Have any of these hindrances compromised the quality of your relationship with God in the past few weeks? If so, describe how.

   ■ Busyness

   ■ Pettiness

   ■ Laziness

   ■ The Cost

2. The author writes, "So what in the end can keep me from coming closer to God? I can! . . . The main problem is that I don't want to be like Jesus, I want to be like me." She says the sinful self is what ultimately prevents us from having a deep relationship with God. With that in mind, read Romans 7:13–8:17 and summarize in the space below the dilemma Paul described.

3. Focus on Romans 8:1-4. How does this encourage you with regard to developing intimacy with God?

4. Now zero in on Romans 8:5-17. List the contrasts between living according to the sinful nature and living according to God's Spirit.

Living according to the sinful nature	*Living according to God's Spirit*

5. What do you think it means to "live according to" either the sinful nature or God's Spirit?

6. How can these truths help you make choices that will strengthen your relationship with God?

Session Six: Listening to God

7. What has God been saying to you through the Scriptures in the last few weeks?

8. What has He taught you through circumstances or other people?

9. How have you responded to what He said?

Session Seven: Keeping the Passion Alive

10. What do the following verses say about how you can keep your passion for Jesus alive?

    ▪ Deuteronomy 30:6

    ▪ Psalm 27:8

    ▪ Proverbs 4:23

11. Look at your answer to question ten (page 81). In the time since you recorded that response, have any of these potential "first loves" competed with Christ for first place in your heart? How?

12. How can you guard your heart against these competing "loves"? Record here what the psalmist asked God to do for him.

    ▪ Psalm 51:10

    ▪ Psalm 86:11

    ▪ Psalm 119:36

    ▪ Psalm 141:4

13.	Write your own prayer to God, confessing any weaknesses you have with competing "loves" and asking Him to help your passion for Christ remain pure and strong. (You may want to end your quiet times this week with this prayer.)

Looking Back, Moving Ahead

14. a. Read James 1:22-25:

> Do not merely listen to the word, and so deceive yourselves. Do what it says. Anyone who listens to the word but does not do what it says is like a man who looks at his face in a mirror and, after looking at himself, goes away and immediately forgets what he looks like. But the man who looks intently into the perfect law that gives freedom, and continues to do this, not forgetting what he has heard, but doing it—he will be blessed in what he does.

b. What responsibilities, stresses, and other factors in your life might tempt you to forget what God has been saying to you through this study? How can you guard against this?

15.	Summarize what you would need to do to "do what it [the Word] says," following the key scriptural truths you've discovered in this study.

Finally, we leave you with some suggestions that can add life and variety to your relationship with God. Read the following twenty suggestions from "**23 Ways to Jump-Start Your Spiritual Battery**" **by Randy Raysbrook** (excerpted from Issue 87). Then put a check mark next to four that you'd like to try in the next month. You can always come back and try the others later! At the end of this section write out your plan and timetable for trying these suggestions.

Ⓓ Bring Vitality to Your Walk

I have found that as my daily spiritual disciplines become mere routine, before long, they can degenerate into empty ritual, and empty ritual into boredom. What can I do to keep my relationship with God fresh, vital, and meaningful?

Sometimes, a change in the way I practice the disciplines brings renewed vitality to my Christian walk. Here are some ways I've discovered to put zest back into my relationship with God.

1. Go on an ego fast.

For a twenty-four-hour period, don't use the words "I," "me," or "mine." When we focus on our egos we squeeze God out of our lives. EGO = Edging God Out.

Ask yourself how much of your conversation (both inner and outer) relates to your needs or desires. Whenever you start to talk about yourself or something you want, consciously choose to focus on others. Draw others out. Choose to focus on their needs or desires, not your own.

2. Dialogue with God about the Ten Commandments.

God revealed His holy character and standards through the Ten Commandments. Pray conversationally about each one. Speak to Him just as you would a good friend. If you pray about the commandment "You shall have no other gods before me" (Exodus 20:3), you might say something like, "Lord, I know You don't want me to make anything in my life more important than You. Yet, at times, I do. I let things crowd You out. But I'm always disappointed when I don't give You first place in my life. Help me identify my idols and destroy them." Don't be in a rush. Wait for His answer. It may prompt new questions or requests on your part.

3. Let God question you.
Our natural tendency is to ask God why He does what He does. For one week allow God to ask you the questions in your quiet time. What would He ask about your time, your secret attitudes, your goals, your pain, or your fears? What are you giving your life to? When we allow God to interrogate us, instead of the other way around, we put Him back in His rightful place as Lord.

4. Hang out with children.
Pray with a small child and observe the simplicity and sincerity of his or her requests. Ask yourself if your prayers are childlike. If they are not, why? ("I tell you the truth, anyone who will not receive the kingdom of God like a little child will never enter it" [Mark 10:15].) Continue to observe children's prayers until you discover new things about your own prayer life.

5. Get to know Jesus as a neighbor.
Imagine that Jesus just moved in next door. Consider what kind of neighbor He might make. What kind of music would He listen to? Who would drop by to visit Him? How would He dress, eat, play? Is it hard to answer these questions? If so, evaluate whether you have an intimate knowledge of Jesus as a person with a distinct personality. You may have a theologically accurate but sterile concept of Him.

6. Read outside your comfort zone.
Try reading religious authors you are not familiar with. Pick up some books representing denominational or theological perspectives different from your own. They may cause you to strengthen your own convictions, develop new ones, or equip you for evangelism. In Acts 17, Paul used his knowledge of pagan Greek poetry to challenge his audience. You don't have to agree with what you read. Try to discover why others believe what they believe.

7. Pray through the newspaper.
As you read the newspaper, pray about people and events. Remember that politics, the law, economics, crime, and social issues all have implications for us as Christians. Paul urged Timothy "that requests, prayers, intercession and thanksgiving be

made for everyone—for kings and all those in authority, that we may live peaceful and quiet lives in all godliness and holiness" (1 Timothy 2:1-2).

We should pray not only for political leaders, but also for cultural leaders. You can also find issues that need prayer in the sports, comic, entertainment, real estate, and travel sections. Instead of frustration or despair, the newspaper should provoke prayer.

8. Set your mind on Christ.
Think about a different role for Christ each day for a week. For example:

Monday—Christ as Deliverer
Tuesday—Christ as Good Shepherd
Wednesday—Christ as Master
Thursday—Christ as Man
Friday—Christ as God
Saturday—Christ as Light
Sunday—Christ as Friend

Meditate throughout each day on Christ's role and what that means to you personally as well as to the rest of mankind. Study the scriptural context in which each of His various names is used. If you find this helpful, consider expanding your week to a month of meditations.

9. Pray with diversity.
Kneeling (Acts 20:36) is only one way to pray. The Bible discusses a variety of ways to approach God. Each has symbolic meaning. Try standing like Jeremiah (Jeremiah 18:20), sitting like David (2 Samuel 7:18), or lying prostrate like Jesus (Matthew 26:39). An attitude of worship can be shown by praying with your face toward the ground (Nehemiah 8:6). Hands lifted up and outstretched toward heaven (Psalm 28:2) can symbolize your desire to reach up to God.

10. WOLEP someone.
We grow fastest when we focus on giving instead of getting. Find someone and WOLEP him. Share something from the Word, a

recent quiet time or memorized verse. *Observe* a need he may have. Look for the subtle as well as the obvious. *Listen* with biblical sensitivity. Draw the person out with good questions. *Encourage* him by helping shoulder his burden. Or tell him what you see God doing in his life. End your time together with *Prayer*.

11. Explore unknown territory.

Select a book of the Bible you have not read or studied and spend time in it. Someone has said that the verses we really need to study are not necessarily the ones we have underlined, but the ones not underlined. It is easy to spend time with sections of the Bible that comfort us; maybe we should spend time with sections that would challenge us.

12. Be like Scrooge.

In *A Christmas Carol*, Scrooge was taken on a trip into the future. Because he saw where he was headed, he was frightened enough to make major changes in his life. Try imagining yourself ten years from now. What do you think your spiritual life will be like then, based on your habits now? Think through your spending habits, thought life, discipling relationships, family relationships, and struggles. We will tend to stay the same and continue to repeat our old habits unless we choose to make changes.

13. Become a historian.

In Nehemiah 9 the Levites reviewed God's historical faithfulness to Israel. They started at creation and worked their way to the present. They cited God's goodness as they remembered their own sinfulness. Why not do the same thing with your life? Review it from the beginning, recalling the times God showed Himself to you. Praise Him as you focus on His attributes and character. Use the Nehemiah prayer as a model, personalizing it: "You are the Lord God, who chose me. Knowing that makes me feel _____(name emotions experienced). I was eager to know You and You made a covenant with me. You gave Israel the Promised Land, Canaan. In the same way, You gave me _____ (name people, thoughts, material goods provided). You have kept Your promise to me by _____ (name His attributes)." Don't feel bound to stay with the format in Nehemiah.

14. Do something in secret.
Richard Foster advises, "Look for ways to serve in hiddenness." There is tremendous blessing in ministering to others without anyone knowing about it. Leave groceries, money, or a gift certificate to a clothing store by the front door of a needy family. Or try doing something anonymously that will encourage someone who is hurting.

15. Take a vow of silence.
Ours is an age of continual noise. God often waits for our souls to still themselves in silence before He speaks. God spoke to Elijah through a gentle whisper (1 Kings 19:11-12). Why not take a temporary vow of silence for twelve to twenty-four hours? Remove yourself, as much as possible, from the noise around you. Try not to speak, consecrate that time to God, and listen intently to Him.

16. Practice consecrated negligence.
Like Martha (Luke 10:38-42), some of us are busy doing so many good things we do not take time to discern what things are needed. Take time to analyze your schedule, for the week and for the month. What are you devoting your time to? What activities have eternal consequences? Determine what you can leave out of your schedule without harm to yourself or others. Choose to neglect those for a period of time. Afterwards, look back and see if it has made a difference in your life. Do this exercise several times a year.

17. Spend a day with your best friend.
Plan a whole day alone with the Lord. If a whole day seems like too much, block off half a day. Think of how you might spend the day with a human friend. Plan a time to share your concerns, needs, or fears. Allow time for just listening and relaxing in God's presence. Catch up on praying about those requests you haven't had time to pray for lately. Pray through some hymns. Read a whole book at a sitting. Pray through verses that you have memorized. Rededicate your life, your job, your family, and your future.

18. Write your own Bible paraphrase.
Choose a favorite book or long passage from the Scriptures. Think deeply about it every day for a week. Pray through it, attack it with questions, cross-reference it, talk about it with others, and read it in

various translations. Think about how you would take these same thoughts and express them to your friends and the current generation. Then write your own personal paraphrase.

19. Take a Bible hike.

Go for a long walk or hike. Before you go, ask God to help you to see everything through a scriptural grid. When you see a tree think of all the verses you know about trees. You may thank God for the beauty of trees in general. Or you may pray about something specifically in those verses. You might end up on a path. What does the Bible say about paths? Things you observe might remind you of concepts referred to in the Bible. A broken limb might remind you of a broken marriage in the church. Raindrops may remind you to thank God for how He nourishes you through fellowship with other believers.

20. Practice redemptive remembrance.

The people of Israel forgot the many times God delivered them: "When our fathers were in Egypt, they gave no thought to your miracles; they did not remember your many kindnesses, and they rebelled by the . . . Red Sea" (Psalm 106:7).

Avoid Israel's sin of not remembering God's many kindnesses. He may have rescued you from physical harm, from foolish decisions, from harmful relationships, or from adverse circumstances. Set aside a time to recall in detail each time He "saved" you and let Him know how you feel about each one. Jot down your memories in a journal, then use them to write your own psalm.

Parting Thought
Whether I realize it or not, I am always in deep, acute need of Jesus Christ. Apart from Him, my nets are always empty, my bucket is always dry. It is when I don't sense that need, when I think I can coast by without Him for a day or two, when I say that my cup is already full—that is when I am in deadly peril.

—Larry Libby, from "Nothing Matters," Issue 66

Grow deeper in all areas of life through these studies from award-winning DISCIPLESHIP JOURNAL.

Following God in Tough Times

Even when we feel imprisoned by life's difficult circumstances, God gives us freedom to choose how we'll respond. Learn how to accept and gain perspective of tough times as you move from survival to service.

Following God in Tough Times
(Michael M. Smith) $6

Beating Busyness

Despite technological advances and enhanced communication, our "to do" lists are longer than ever. Identify and tackle stressful issues in your life through this study based on excerpts from top *Discipleship Journal* articles and related exercises.

Beating Busyness
(Adam Holz) $6

Becoming More Like Jesus

Becoming like Jesus is a process, not just learning a list of rules. Based on excerpts from top *Discipleship Journal* articles, this study will help you develop His character in you as you evaluate your life, understand Jesus' teachings on character, and live them out.

Becoming More Like Jesus
(Michael M. Smith) $6

Discipleship Journal's 101 Best Small-Group Ideas

Pulled from fifteen years of the best *Discipleship Journal* articles, these fun and practical ideas will help your group grow in areas like outreach, serving, prayer, Bible study, and more!

Discipleship Journal's 101 Best Small-Group Ideas $11

Get your copies today at your local bookstore, through our website, or by calling (800) 366-7788.
(Ask for offer **#2335** or a FREE catalog of NavPress products.)

NAVPRESS
BRINGING TRUTH TO LIFE
www.navpress.com

Prices subject to change.